Gold Rush

by Eric Kraft

Table of Contents

Gold

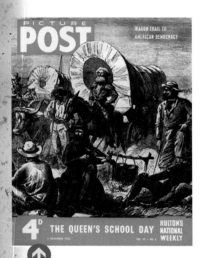

Magazines such as the *Picture Post* kept people informed about the Gold Rush.

"Gold! Gold! Gold from the American River!" the man shouted as he ran through the streets of San Francisco, California. He was carrying a bottle of gold dust. People rushed to the spot, ready to take risks and work hard in the hope of striking it rich.

The years from 1849 to 1900 were a time of great gold rushes in the United States. A gold rush is a sudden movement of a large number of people to a place where gold has been found. Men and women left their homes and traveled hundreds, sometimes even thousands, of miles to get to the gold fields. They faced huge obstacles, and most failed to become rich. But the thought of finding gold kept them coming!

Like this miner, many people were anxious to join in a gold rush to get rich quickly.

Gold has been a valuable metal since ancient times. Its color and **luster** are part of its attraction. Jewelry makers have always found working with gold easier than working with any other metal. Gold conducts electricity well, so it is used in some of the tiny circuits inside the most powerful computers.

However, the main reason gold is so highly valued is the simple fact that there isn't much of it. Because it is rare and hard to find, gold has been used as money or as the **standard** by which money is valued.

In the days of the gold rushes, money often took the form of ingots. Ingots are molds that can take any shape, including rectangular bars and circular coins.

Miners take a rest at the Pandora Mine in Telluride, Colorado.

In Their Own Words

From a letter written by a gold miner in Placerville, California, dated October 1850:

"I have left those that I love as my own life behind & risked every thing and endured many hardships to get here, & I want to make enough to live easier...My great anxiety is for my wife & child. I cannot hear from them. The last time I heard from them was dated the 14 August."

The people looking for gold were called **prospectors**. A prospector's dream was to "strike it rich," or find lots of gold. Some prospectors did strike it rich, but most did not. They worked long and hard for very little return.

Often the people who really struck it rich during gold rushes were not miners. They were the people who made the equipment that the miners used. They were store owners who sold goods and supplies to prospectors at high prices.

The gold rushes brought thousands of people to the places where gold had been discovered. People gave up their jobs to try their luck in the hunt for gold.

The people hoping to strike it rich often left their families behind. They planned to bring their riches home to their families. However, many who came to California, Colorado, Nevada, and Alaska in search of gold stayed. Instead of returning to their families, they brought their families to them. In doing so, they turned mining camps into settled towns.

IT'S A FACT!

- In 1849, about 90,000 people left their homes to go to California in search of gold.
- In 1850, another 85,000 joined them.
- In 1859, nearly 100,000 people rushed to Colorado seeking gold.
- In 1897, as many as 100,000 set out for the Klondike after gold was discovered there. However, only about 40,000 made the entire trip.

The Gold Rush turned San Francisco into a thriving town and an important place for buying and selling gold.

5

Time Line of the Gold Rush

The Mexican War ends. The Rio Grande is made the southern boundary of Texas, and California and New Mexico are ceded to the United States. Gold is discovered in California.

California is admitted to the Union as a nonslave state.

The Republican party is established.

Running for the Senate from Illinois, Abraham Lincoln debates Stephen A. Douglas, opposing slavery. Gold seekers rush to Colorado when gold is found there.

| 1848 | 1849 | 1850 | 1852 | 1854 | 1857 | 1858 | 1859 |

Eighty thousand gold seekers rush to California.

Harriet Beecher Stowe's novel, Uncle Tom's Cabin, is published.

The Supreme Court upholds slavery in the Dred Scott decision.

The abolitionist John Brown stages his uprising. Gold and silver are discovered at the Comstock Lode in Nevada.

135,000 SETS, 270,000 VOLUMES SOLD.

UNCLE TOM'S CABIN

FOR SALE HERE.

AN EDITION FOR THE MILLION, COMPLETE IN 1 Vol., PRICE 37 1-2 CENTS.
IN GERMAN, IN 1 Vol. PRICE 50 CENTS.
IN 2 Vols, CLOTH, 6 PLATES, PRICE $1.50.
SUPERB ILLUSTRATED EDITION, IN 1 Vol. WITH 153 ENGRAVINGS,
PRICES FROM $2.50 TO $5.00.

The Greatest Book of the Age.

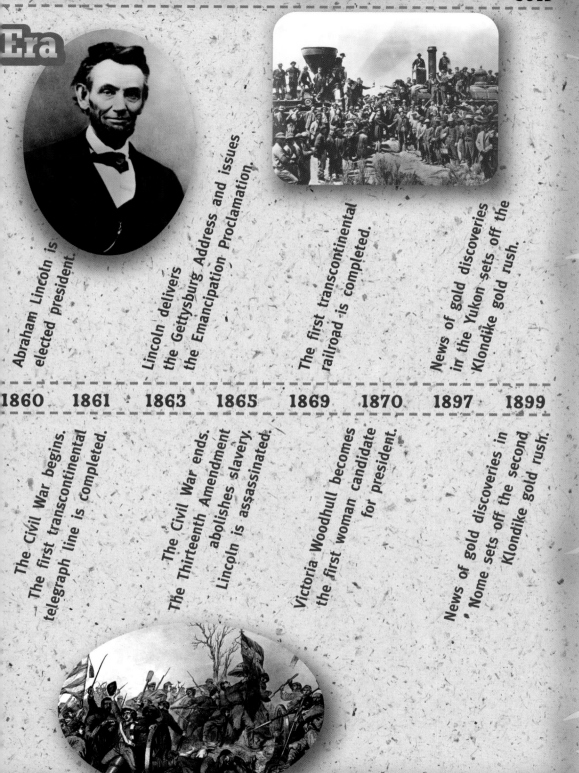

Era

Abraham Lincoln is elected president.

Lincoln delivers the Gettysburg Address and issues the Emancipation Proclamation.

The first transcontinental railroad is completed.

News of gold discoveries in the Yukon sets off the Klondike gold rush.

| 1860 | 1861 | 1863 | 1865 | 1869 | 1870 | 1897 | 1899 |

The Civil War begins. The first transcontinental telegraph line is completed.

The Civil War ends. The Thirteenth Amendment abolishes slavery. Lincoln is assassinated.

Victoria Woodhull becomes the first woman candidate for president.

News of gold discoveries in Nome sets off the second Klondike gold rush.

The California 49ers

Johann Sutter was a Swiss **immigrant** who built his home on land that is today Sacramento. His little empire had vast acres of farmland and as many buildings as a small town. James Marshall was one of Sutter's employees. In January 1848, he discovered gold while building a sawmill for Sutter on the American River.

For quite a while, the discovery was kept a secret. Then, in the spring, a man named Sam Brannan let the secret out. He went through the streets shouting "Gold! Gold!" Nearly all the 800 residents of the town rushed off in search of gold.

Sutter's Mill was the place where gold was first discovered on January 24, 1848.

The rest of the country knew nothing about it. News did not travel fast or easily at that time. There were no telegraph lines. There was no railroad that linked California with the rest of the country. Ships traveling from the West Coast to the East Coast took six months to get around the southern tip of South America.

In December 1848, President James Polk assured the country that there really was gold in California. The rush was on. People from all over headed to California, hoping to strike it rich.

IT'S A FACT!

Because the California Gold Rush actually started in 1849, the gold seekers became known as 49ers.

Crowded with men looking to make their fortunes from the Gold Rush, ships sailed around Cape Horn on their way to California to complete the six-month journey.

Gold seekers coming from the East Coast had a choice of three routes, none of them easy. They could sail by ship around South America. That journey took about six months and included the dangerous passage around Cape Horn, at the southern tip of South America. There the weather was stormy and the sea was very rough.

They could sail by ship to Panama. Then they had to cross Panama. They made the crossing partly by canoe, partly by mule or horse, and partly on foot. When they reached the Pacific Ocean, they waited for a ship to take them to San Francisco. This route might take as little as eight weeks, but there was great danger of disease.

In Their Own Words

From the *Personal Memoirs* of Ulysses S. Grant: "The fortunate could go by Cape Horn or by the Isthmus of Panama; but the mass of pioneers crossed the plains with their ox teams. This took an entire summer."

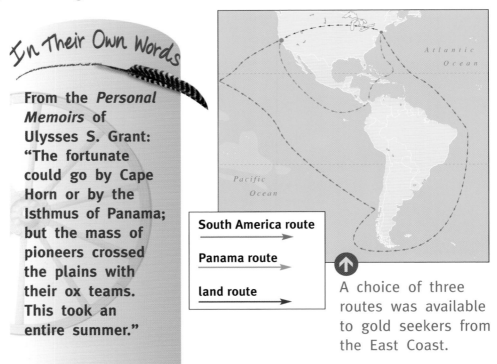

South America route

Panama route

land route

A choice of three routes was available to gold seekers from the East Coast.

They could travel by land across the **prairies** and mountains of the United States. If they were lucky, there would be trails they could follow to the California Trail, which was a major trail west. Native Americans along the way often helped the gold seekers find food. However, the disease cholera killed many of those who took the land routes.

Life was difficult for gold prospectors. Here a miner prepares a meal over a campfire. His burro carries all his possessions and equipment.

When gold was discovered, there were about 14,000 settlers in California. By the end of 1849, there were almost 100,000. In three more years, the population grew to about 250,000.

During that time, the average worker in the East might make $1 a day. A fairly good—and lucky— gold miner in California might make $8 a day. But the gold miner had to contend with a high cost of living. As people poured into California, prices for food and supplies increased. A worker in New York could buy a loaf of bread for 4 cents. The California miner had to pay 75 cents. Eggs cost $1 to $3 each. Apples sold for $1 to $5 each.

Point

Talk About It

Sam Brannan was the man who ran through the streets of Sacramento shouting that gold had been discovered. He never prospected for gold, but he did make a lot of money from the Gold Rush by selling shovels. Why do you think Brannan became rich selling shovels?

A pick, a shovel, and a pan were important tools for the typical gold miner.

Chinese gold seekers also came to California. They rarely got rich.

Most of the miners hoped to find gold by a method called "placer" mining. The name comes from a Spanish word for "sand bank." Placer miners looked for bits of gold that had washed out of deep underground deposits. They often looked in the sandy bottoms and banks of rivers and streams.

Placer mining was hard work, but it didn't require a lot of costly equipment. A person could wash sand in a pan, looking for the flecks of gold that might be hidden in it. This was called panning for gold. A more efficient method was to pour water over sand in a cradle, a wooden box mounted on rockers. When the cradle was rocked, the gold fell to the bottom.

↑ Where there were no towns, miners lived in camps. They often gave these camps colorful names, such as Angel's Camp, Gold Hill, Poorman Creek, Poverty Hill, Red Dog, Roaring Camp, and Rough and Ready.

In Their Own Words

Joseph Wood joined the Gold Rush in the summer of 1849. That winter, he wrote this to his family:
"To sum up the whole matter of our winter's labor so far, we have made nothing."
The next spring, feeling beaten, he wrote this:
"I am lonesome this cold dark rainy night...I would give an ounce [of gold] to crawl into my old bed at home and remain there until morning."

By the end of 1849, most of the easy-to-find gold was gone. However, people kept coming to California in search of gold. Life in the mining camps became dangerous. Those who had not struck it rich often blamed their failure on others. Fights broke out between people of different races or **ethnic groups**. Disease, starvation, accidents, and violence killed many miners and drove many more back home.

By 1852, the boom was over. Not many miners had made their fortunes. Placer mining worked for only a few. Most of the gold was deep in the ground. Only people with the money to buy expensive mining equipment and hire many miners could find it and dig it out.

The most important and most lasting effect of the Gold Rush of 1849 was that it made California famous around the world. People now thought of California as a place to strike it rich, one way or another. They continued to arrive, seeking a better life.

In Their Own Words

Johann Sutter felt that the Gold Rush ruined him. In his diary, he wrote: "All my plans and projects came to naught. One after another, all my people disappeared in the direction of the gold fields. My property was entirely exposed and at the mercy of the rabble...I was alone and there was no law." Squatters took possession of his land, and he never got it back.

These three miners prospected in Rockerville, South Dakota, where $350,000 worth of gold was discovered between 1876 and 1878.

Pikes Peak or Bust

The discovery of gold in California led people to search for gold in other parts of the West. Ten years later, the 49ers were replaced by the 59ers who headed to Colorado to find gold.

Pikes Peak can be seen from as far away as Kansas. Many gold seekers came from Kansas and could keep the peak in sight for the entire journey.

In 1858, William Green Russell found gold where the South Platte River and Cherry Creek came together, near what is now Denver. The place is about 70 miles (112 kilometers) north of the mountain called Pikes Peak. Thousands of people around the country declared "Pikes Peak or Bust" and headed for Colorado. They had the same hope that had driven the 49ers—the hope of striking it rich.

During the years 1858 and 1859, about 50,000 people came to Colorado hoping to find gold. At the time, Cherry Creek divided two small communities, Denver City and Aurora. The huge numbers of new arrivals overwhelmed the two small communities. In 1860, they merged as the city of Denver.

A miner panning for gold in Colorado during the gold rush there. ➡

There wasn't much gold to be found in the area near Denver. But there were other gold strikes elsewhere in Colorado. There were strikes at Idaho Springs, Central City, and Cripple Creek. These strikes kept eager gold seekers coming in the hope of finding gold. Some people struck it rich by taking advantage of gold seekers. These people, called **outfitters**, sold packages that were supposed to include supplies and transportation from the cities and towns along the Mississippi River where the trails began.

In Their Own Words

Gold seeker T. S. Kenderdine wrote: "When I crossed the plains...the City of Denver was not laid out, and the gold finds on Cherry Creek, while known in the East, were unheard of along the California Trail. The prairie schooner, with "Pike's Peak or Bust" charcoaled on its cover, had been there and returned, with the lettering replaced with Busted. The people are roughly dressed and the children run wild."

Railroad companies often provided lists of materials a group of four men journeying west would need.

INTRODUCTION.

It was not the intention of the compilers of this map to add a Guide, but from the numerous incidents which have lately sprung up regarding the Gold fields of Western Kansas, they found it impossible to lay down the location of every place which they deemed useful without rendering the topographical part crowded and indistinct. They have therefore introduced a few pages, giving the neccessary outfit for four men, six months in the mines; the distances to the principal camping places along the routes; and also the different mail stations &c. along the route to California.

List of outfits for four men six months.

TEAM, WAGON AND FIXTURES:

2 Yoke of Oxen	$120.00
1 Wagon	65.00
Wagon-Cover, Yokes and chains	10.00
	$195.00

TOOLS:

4 Steel Picks with handles	$5.00
4 Shovels	3.00
1 Pit Saw	7.00
2 Axes	2.00
1 Hatchet	65
1 Saw File	25
2 Gold Pans	1.50
1 Chisel	30
1 Auger	25
1 Hand Saw	1.00
1 Drawing Knife	50
25 ℔ of Nails @ 5cts.	1.25
2 Gimlets	15
2 ℔ Quicksilver and retort	3.00
Sheet Iron for Long Toms	75
	$26.60

CAMP FIXTURES AND FURNITURE:

8 Pair of Blankets	$24.00
1 Camp Kettle	1.00
4 Tin Plates	30
4 Spoons	15
1 Coffee Pot	50
1 Camp Stand	1.00
4 Cups	35
1 Dipper	15
1 Large Spoon	15
1 Frying Pan	35
1 Dutch Oven	70
1 Bread Pan	30
1 Coffee Mill	40
1 Wooden Bucket	25
4 Knives	1.00
	$30.75

PROVISIONS:

6 Sacks of Flour at $3	$18.00
400 ℔ of Bacon at 10cts.	40.00
100 ℔ of Coffee at 11cts.	11.00
6 ℔ of Tea at 75cts.	4.50
100 ℔ of Sugar at 7cts.	7.00
100 ℔ of Salt	1.00
6 ℔ Ground Pepper	1.00
1 Ten Gallon Water Keg	1.00
2 Bushels of Dried Fruit	2.50
2 Bushels of Beans	2.00
250 ℔ Pilot Bread @ 5cts.	12.50
1 Bushel of Rice	1.50
1 Box of Soap	1.00
	$103.00
Team	195.00
Tools	26.60
Camp Fixtures	30.75
	$355.85

SUNDRIES:

3 Gallons of Brandy,
12 ℔ Gunpowder,
25 ℔ of Lead,
10 ℔ of Shot,
2000 Gun Caps,
2 dozen Box of Matches,
15 ℔ of Candles,
1 Whet Stone

Because an expedition to the gold fields was difficult and dangerous, life insurance was popular. Companies advertised their policies.

PIKE'S PEAK GOLD REGIONS! LIFE INSURANCE!
Policies granted by
THE NEW-YORK LIFE INSURANCE CO.
112 & 114 Broadway, N.Y.
ACCUMULATED CAPITAL
ONE MILLION, SIX HUNDRED THOUSAND DOLLARS

In view of the extensive emigration to the Gold Regions, the above well-known Company of 14 years standing, are now prepared to issue policies for that locality. Parties can thus secure to their families or friends some resource in case of accidents, and creditors protect themselves from loss for advances. For full particulars, as of Rates, &c., apply to

J. W. Jennings, Agent, at *Mercer*

With Pikes Peak in sight, a mining party makes its way toward the gold fields.

Some outfitters made the journey seem quick and easy. They **underestimated** the distance. Some didn't supply enough food and water for the entire journey. Many gold seekers quit in disgust without ever reaching the gold fields.

Gold mining was difficult in Colorado because the gold was in rugged mountain areas. Much of it had to be dug out of the ground with costly equipment. Once again, few miners struck it rich. Companies that could buy heavy equipment made the money.

The Comstock Lode

The gold rushes in California and Colorado brought tens of thousands of gold seekers to the West. Other small discoveries of gold kept many of them there. These discoveries also encouraged others to head west to strike it rich.

In 1859, prospectors struck gold in an area of Nevada near the California border. The richest strike was in Six-Mile Canyon, near the town now called Virginia City. It became known as the Comstock Lode because prospector Henry T. P. Comstock staked the first claim to the land. When news of the strike got out, miners who had yet to strike it rich in California or Colorado rushed to the Comstock Lode.

a mine office in Virginia City, Nevada

Finding gold in Nevada was difficult because of the composition of the mud.

The miners found that digging for gold in that area was very hard. The gold was mixed in with a thick, gray mud, and it was hard to separate the gold from the mud. When the heavy mud was **analyzed** to determine its makeup, results showed it to be rich in silver. The Nevada gold strike turned out to be the richest silver strike in the United States.

A flutter wheel was one of the devices prospectors used to mine gold and silver.

Once again, very few of the small-scale miners made much money. The gold and silver were buried deep in the ground. Mining in Nevada required expensive equipment and teams of workers to dig deep shafts and tunnels. Only the few who could afford to buy the machinery and hire the miners struck it rich.

Some of those people had already made fortunes in California. They used their money to set up mining companies that could get the gold and silver out of the ground. Those who made fortunes were nicknamed the "Bonanza Kings."

The Civil War was raging at the time of the Comstock strike. President Abraham Lincoln needed gold and silver from the mines to pay the costs of the war. He also wanted to increase the number of states fighting for the Union. So he urged Congress to accept Nevada as a state. He did this despite the fact that Nevada did not have enough residents to qualify. Lincoln signed a **bill** making Nevada a state in 1864.

Towns could grow practically overnight as eager gold seekers rushed to strike it rich. If the gold wasn't there, or if there was less than the miners had hoped, the towns could be abandoned just as quickly. Some of these abandoned towns, or gold-rush ghost towns, dot the West today.

The Klondike

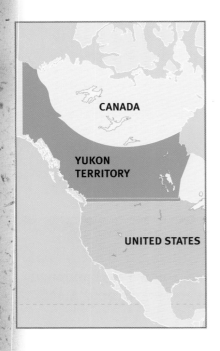

In August 1896, three prospectors found gold in a **tributary** of the Klondike River in Canada's Yukon Territory. By 1897, news of the discoveries reached Seattle, Washington, and set off a rush of gold seekers.

These new gold strikes were a long distance away for gold miners in the United States. The Yukon was more than 2,000 miles (3,200 kilometers) northwest of Seattle. The weather was fierce. It was a rugged area in which winter cold could cause a person to freeze to death in just minutes. Ships became stuck in frozen harbors.

Many women went to the Klondike in search of gold. Many others sought their fortunes in business. Some ran hotels. Others sold supplies. Martha Black came seeking gold. She climbed the Dyea Trail, prospected for gold, and then ran a sawmill. Years later she was elected as a representative to Canada's House of Parliament.

Seattle became the departure point for the tens of thousands who set out for the Yukon. Most journeyed by ship to the towns of Skagway and Dyea. From there, they hiked inland over mountainous trails packed with snow. Many died. Many more gave up and turned back.

The Dyea Trail led over the Chilkoot Pass to the gold fields inland. One part of the trail, known as the Golden Stairs, was 1,500 steep steps carved in ice. Many miners reaching the Stairs returned home after taking one look!

From a prospectors' camp, tens of thousands of hopeful people began the exhausting trek to the gold fields.

A group of actresses were photographed as they crossed the Dyea River on their way to the new boom towns in the Klondike where gold had been discovered. Their performances provided prospectors with much needed entertainment after a long day of mining.

Many of those who journeyed to the Yukon were foolishly unprepared for what they would face. They had no experience with Yukon weather. They didn't know their way around the area. They didn't have the right gear or enough supplies.

After some miners died, Canada took action to ensure greater safety. Only those prospectors with enough supplies, including food, to last a year were allowed to enter the country.

Travel in the Yukon was very difficult. Horses and mules couldn't climb the icy trails. Many miners carried their supplies themselves. Carrying a year's worth of supplies meant making many trips. The miner would go back and forth over a short section of the trail, moving the supplies in batches. When everything had been moved, the **process** would begin all over again for the next short section of the trail. Working this way, a miner might need three months to make the 35-mile trip over the mountains from Skagway or Dyea.

IT'S A FACT!

Horses and mules weren't suited to the Klondike. Their hooves sank in the snow, and their weight could break through the ice on frozen rivers. Prospectors turned to dogs to pull the sleds that carried them and their gear. A team of dogs was hitched to a sled. One dog was trained to be the lead dog. It kept the other dogs pulling together.

The snowy lands of the Klondike were not welcoming, but for prospectors, they were a temporary home.

Gold seekers often roped themselves together in order to climb the mountains of the Klondike.

The cold and the rough terrain didn't discourage gold seekers. They kept coming to the Klondike—or at least they tried to make the trip. More than 100,000 people started out for the Klondike. Most of them bought their supplies and gear in Seattle. As a result, Seattle grew into a boom town. Many shopkeepers there made their fortunes without ever leaving home. Of the 100,000 people who tried to reach the gold fields, only about 30,000 made it.

By the time most of the gold seekers reached the gold fields, it was too late. Those who had arrived there first had claimed most of the valuable land. The lucky few, the "Klondike Kings," became very rich. The others did not. Most of them wound up working for the lucky ones.

When the easy-to-find gold was gone, Klondike mining became hard work. Miners had to dig deep through the frozen ground to get to the gold.

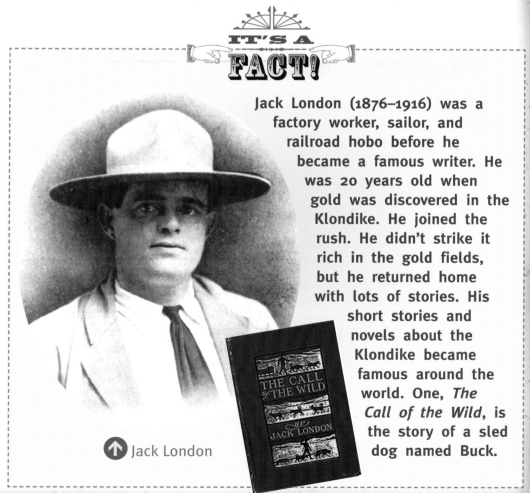

IT'S A FACT!

Jack London (1876–1916) was a factory worker, sailor, and railroad hobo before he became a famous writer. He was 20 years old when gold was discovered in the Klondike. He joined the rush. He didn't strike it rich in the gold fields, but he returned home with lots of stories. His short stories and novels about the Klondike became famous around the world. One, *The Call of the Wild*, is the story of a sled dog named Buck.

⬆ Jack London

By 1899, the original Klondike rush was over. There was news of a new strike in Nome, Alaska. What did people do when they heard the news? They packed up and rushed to Nome, of course, hoping to strike it rich.

The gold rushes formed an important and exciting episode in U.S. history. Lured by the prospect of getting rich quickly and easily, and encouraged by a spirit of courage and adventure, the gold seekers ventured forth by the thousands.

Point

Think It Over

Why do you think people rushed from gold strike to gold strike when the chance of finding gold was so slim?

The possibility of finding gold and getting rich quick kept the miners traveling from place to place.

Glossary

analyze	(AN-uh-lize) to study something carefully (page 21)
bill	(BIHL) a proposed law that a legislative body votes to approve or not (page 23)
ethnic group	(ETH-nihk GROOP) people with the same cultural background (page 14)
immigrant	(IM-uh-grent) a person who moves from one country to live in another (page 8)
luster	(LUH-stur) a glow of reflected light (page 3)
outfitter	(OUT-fiht-er) a person who sold packages that were supposed to include supplies and transportation for gold seekers (page 18)
prairie	(PRAER-ee) vast grassland in the central part of the United States (page 11)
process	(PRAH-sess) a set of steps to accomplish something (page 27)
prospector	(PRAH-spek-tur) a person who looks for a valuable natural resource (page 4)
standard	(STAND-urd) something by which another thing is measured (page 3)
tributary	(TRIH-byoo-tare-ee) a smaller river that flows into a larger one (page 24)
underestimate	(UN-dur-EST-uh-mayt) to think of something as less than it is (page 19)

Index